DEPARTMENT OF THE TREASURY
TECHNICAL EXPLANATION OF THE PROTOCOL
SIGNED AT WASHINGTON ON SEPTEMBER 30, 2005
AMENDING THE CONVENTION BETWEEN
THE UNITED STATES OF AMERICA
AND
THE GOVERNMENT OF SWEDEN
FOR THE AVOIDANCE OF DOUBLE TAXATION AND
THE PREVENTION OF FISCAL EVASION
WITH RESPECT TO TAXES ON INCOME,
SIGNED AT WASHINGTON ON SEPTEMBER 1, 1994

DEPARTMENT OF THE TREASURY
TECHNICAL EXPLANATION OF THE PROTOCOL
SIGNED AT WASHINGTON ON SEPTEMBER 30, 2005
AMENDING THE CONVENTION BETWEEN
THE UNITED STATES OF AMERICA
AND
THE GOVERNMENT OF SWEDEN
FOR THE AVOIDANCE OF DOUBLE TAXATION AND
THE PREVENTION OF FISCAL EVASION
WITH RESPECT TO TAXES ON INCOME,
SIGNED AT WASHINGTON ON SEPTEMBER 1, 1994

This is a technical explanation of the Protocol signed at Washington on September 30, 2005 (the "Protocol"), amending the Convention between the United States of America and the Government of Sweden for the avoidance of double taxation and the prevention of fiscal evasion with respect to taxes on income, signed at Washington on September 1, 1994 (the "Convention").

Negotiations took into account the U.S. Department of the Treasury's current tax treaty policy and Treasury's Model Income Tax Convention, published on September 20, 1996 (the "U.S. Model"). Negotiations also took into account the Model Tax Convention on Income and on Capital, published by the Organization for Economic Cooperation and Development (the "OECD Model"), and recent tax treaties concluded by both countries.

This Technical Explanation is an official guide to the Protocol. It explains policies behind particular provisions, as well as understandings reached during the negotiations with respect to the interpretation and application of the Protocol. This technical explanation is not intended to provide a complete guide to the Convention as amended by the Protocol. To the extent that the Convention has not been amended by the Protocol, the Technical Explanation of the Convention remains the official explanation. References in this technical explanation to "he" or "his" should be read to mean "he or she" or "his or her."

Article I

Article I of the Protocol modifies Article 1 (Personal Scope) of the Convention with respect to the last sentence of paragraph 4, which permits the United States to tax as U.S. citizens former citizens whose loss of citizenship had as one of its principal purposes the avoidance of tax. To reflect 1996 and 2004 amendments to U.S. tax law in this area, the Protocol provides that, notwithstanding other provisions of the Convention, a former citizen or long-term resident of the United States may, for the period of ten years following the loss of such status, be taxed in accordance with the laws of the United States.

Section 877 of the Internal Revenue Code of 1986 (the "Code") generally applies to a former citizen or long-term resident of the United States who relinquishes citizenship or terminates long-term residency if either of the following criteria exceed established thresholds: (a) the average annual net income tax of such individual for the period of 5 taxable years ending before the date of the loss of status, or (b) the net worth of such individual as of the date of the loss of status. The thresholds are adjusted annually for inflation. The United States defines "long-term resident" as an individual (other than a U.S. citizen) who is a lawful permanent resident of the United States in at least 8 of the prior 15 taxable years. An individual is not treated as a lawful permanent resident for any taxable year if such individual is treated as a resident of a foreign country under the provisions of a tax treaty between the United States and the foreign country and the individual does not waive the benefits of such treaty applicable to residents of the foreign country.

Paragraph b) of Article I of the Protocol also addresses special issues presented by fiscally transparent entities such as partnerships and certain trusts and estates. In general, paragraph b) of Article I relates to entities that are not subject to tax at the entity level, as distinct from entities that are subject to tax, but with respect to which tax may be relieved under an integrated system. This paragraph applies to any resident of a Contracting State who is entitled to income derived through an entity that is treated as fiscally transparent under the laws of either Contracting State. Entities falling under this description in the United States include partnerships, common investment trusts under section 584 and grantor trusts. This paragraph also applies to U.S. limited liability companies ("LLCs") that are treated as partnerships for U.S. tax purposes.

Under paragraph b) of Article I of the Protocol, an item of income, profit or gain derived by such a fiscally transparent entity will be considered to be derived by a resident of a Contracting State if a resident is treated under the taxation laws of that State as deriving the item of income. For example, if a Swedish company pays interest to an entity that is treated as fiscally transparent for U.S. tax purposes, the interest will be considered derived by a resident of the U.S. only to the extent that the taxation laws of the United States treats one or more U.S. residents (whose status as U.S. residents is determined, for this purpose, under U.S. tax law) as deriving the interest for U.S. tax purposes. In the case of a partnership, the persons who are, under U.S. tax laws, treated as partners of the entity would normally be the persons whom the U.S. tax laws would treat as deriving the interest income through the partnership. Also, it follows that persons whom the United States treats as partners but who are not U.S. residents for U.S. tax purposes may not claim a benefit for the interest paid to the entity under the Convention, because they are not residents of the United States for purposes of claiming this treaty benefit. (If, however, the country in which they are treated as resident for tax purposes, as determined under the laws of that country, has an income tax convention with Sweden, they may be entitled to claim a benefit under that convention.) In contrast, if, for example, an entity is organized under U.S. laws and is classified as a corporation for U.S. tax purposes, interest paid by a Swedish company to the U.S. entity will be considered derived by a resident of the United States since the U.S. corporation is treated under U.S. taxation laws as a resident of the United States and as deriving the income.

The same result obtains even if the entity were viewed differently under the tax laws of the country of source (*e.g.*, as not fiscally transparent in Sweden in the first example above where the entity is treated as a partnership for U.S. tax purposes). Similarly, the characterization of the entity in a third country is also irrelevant, even if the entity is organized in that third country. The results follow regardless of whether the entity is disregarded as a separate entity under the laws of one jurisdiction but not the other, such as a single owner entity that is viewed as a branch for U.S. tax purposes and as a corporation for Swedish tax purposes. These results also obtain regardless of where the entity is organized (*i.e.*, in the United States, in Sweden, or, as noted above, in a third country).

For example, income from U.S. sources received by an entity organized under the laws of the United States, which is treated for Swedish tax purposes as a corporation and is owned by a Swedish shareholder who is a Swedish resident for Swedish tax purposes, is not considered derived by the shareholder of that corporation even if, under the tax laws of the United States, the entity is treated as fiscally transparent. Rather, for purposes of the treaty, the income is treated as derived by the U.S. entity.

Article II

Article II of the Protocol modifies Article 2 (Taxes Covered) of the Convention by replacing subparagraph b) of paragraph 1, which identifies the Swedish taxes to which the Convention applies. Subparagraph b) of paragraph 1 applies to the following Swedish taxes: (1) the national income tax, (2) the withholding tax on dividends, (3) the income tax on non-residents, (4) the income tax on non-resident artistes and athletes, (5) the national capital tax (for purposes of paragraph 3 of Article 2), (6) the excise tax on insurance premiums paid to foreign insurers, and (7) the municipal income tax.

Article III

Article III of the Protocol replaces paragraph 1 of Article 4 (Residence) of the Convention. The term "resident of a Contracting State" is defined in subparagraph a) of paragraph 1. In general, this definition incorporates the definitions of residence in U.S. and Swedish law by referring to a resident as a person who, under the laws of a Contracting State, is subject to tax there by reason of his domicile, residence, citizenship, place of management, place of incorporation or any other similar criterion and also includes that State and any political subdivision or local authority thereof. Thus, residents of the United States include aliens who are considered U.S. residents under Code section 7701(b). Subparagraphs b) and c) address special cases that may arise in the context of Article 4.

Certain entities that are nominally subject to tax but that in practice are rarely required to pay tax also would generally be treated as residents and therefore accorded treaty benefits. For example, a U.S. Regulated Investment Company (RIC), U.S. Real Estate Investment Trust (REIT) and U.S. Real Estate Mortgage Investment Conduit are all residents of the United States for purposes of the treaty. Although the income earned by these entities normally is not subject to U.S. tax in the hands of the entity, they are taxable to the extent that they do not currently distribute their profits, and therefore may be regarded as "liable to tax." They also must satisfy a number of requirements under the Code in order to be entitled to special tax treatment.

A person who is liable to tax in a Contracting State only in respect of income from sources within that State or capital situated therein or of profits attributable to a permanent establishment in that State will not be treated as a resident of that Contracting State for purposes of the Convention. Thus, a consular official of Sweden who is posted in the United States, who may be subject to U.S. tax on U.S. source investment income, but is not taxable in the United States on non-U.S. source income, would not be considered a resident of the United States for purposes of the Convention. (See Code section 7701(b)(5)(B)). Similarly, an enterprise of Sweden with a permanent establishment in the United States is not, by virtue of that permanent establishment, a resident of the United States. The enterprise generally is subject to U.S. tax only with respect to its income that is attributable to the U.S. permanent establishment, not with respect to its worldwide income, as it would be if it were a U.S. resident.

Subparagraph b) of paragraph 1 contains an exception to the general rule of paragraph 1 a) that residence under internal law also determines residence under the Convention. The exception applies with respect to a U.S. citizen or alien lawfully admitted for permanent residence (*i.e.*, a "green card" holder). Under paragraph 1 a), a person is considered a resident of the United States for purposes of the Convention if he is liable to tax in the United States by reason of citizenship. In addition, aliens admitted to the United States for permanent residence ("green card" holders) qualify as U.S. residents under the first sentence of paragraph 1 because they are taxed by the United States as residents, regardless of where they physically reside.

Under the exception of paragraph 1 b), a U.S. citizen or green card holder will be treated as a resident of the United States for purposes of the Convention, and, thereby entitled to treaty benefits, only if he has a substantial presence (see section 7701(b)(3)), permanent home or habitual abode in the United States. This rule requires that the U.S. citizen or green card holder have a reasonably strong economic nexus with the United States. If such a person is a resident of both the United States and Sweden, whether or not he is to be treated as a resident of the United States for purposes of the Convention is determined by the tie-breaker rules of paragraph 2.

Thus, for example, an individual resident of Mexico who is a U.S. citizen by birth, or who is a Mexican citizen and holds a U.S. green card, but who, in either case, has never lived in the United States, would not be entitled to benefits under the Convention. However, a U.S. citizen who is transferred to Mexico for two years would be entitled to benefits under the Convention if he maintains a permanent home or habitual abode in the United States and is not a resident of Mexico for purposes of the Sweden-Mexico tax treaty.

The fact that a U.S. citizen who does not have close ties to the United States may not be treated as a U.S. resident under the Convention does not alter the application of the saving clause of paragraph 4 of Article 1 (Personal Scope) to that citizen. For example, a U.S. citizen who pursuant to the "citizen/green card holder" rule is not considered to be a resident of the United States still is taxable on his worldwide income under the generally applicable rules of the Code.

Subparagraph (c) of paragraph 1 of Article 4 of the Convention provides that certain tax-exempt entities such as pension funds and charitable organizations will be regarded as residents of a Contracting State regardless of whether they are generally liable to income tax in the State where they are established. Subparagraph (c) applies to legal persons organized under the laws of a Contracting State and established and maintained in that State: to provide pensions or other similar benefits pursuant to a plan; or exclusively for religious, charitable, scientific, artistic, cultural, or educational purposes and that is a resident of a Contracting State. Thus, an exempt section 501(c) organization (such as a U.S. charity) that is generally exempt from tax under U.S. law is a resident of the United States for all purposes of the Convention.

Article IV

Article IV of the Protocol replaces Article 10 (Dividends) of the Convention. Article 10 provides rules for the taxation of dividends paid by a company that is a resident of one Contracting State to a beneficial owner that is a resident of the other Contracting State. The Article provides for full residence country taxation of such dividends and a limited source-State right to tax.

Paragraph 1

The right of a shareholder's country of residence to tax dividends arising in the source country is preserved by paragraph 1, which permits a Contracting State to tax its residents on dividends paid to them by a company that is a resident of the other Contracting State.

Paragraph 2

The State of source also may tax dividends beneficially owned by a resident of the other State, subject to the limitations of paragraphs 2 and 3. Paragraph 2 generally limits the tax in the State of source on the dividend paid by a company resident in that State to 15 percent of the gross amount of the dividend. If, however, the beneficial owner of the dividend is a company that is a resident of the other State and that directly owns shares representing at least 10 percent of the voting power of the company paying the dividend, then the withholding tax in the State of source is limited to 5 percent of the gross amount of the dividend. Shares are considered voting shares if they provide the power to elect, appoint or replace any person vested with the powers ordinarily exercised by the board of directors of a U.S. corporation.

The benefits of paragraph 2 may be granted at the time of payment by means of reduced withholding at source. It also is consistent with the paragraph for tax to be withheld at the time of payment at full statutory rates, and the treaty benefit to be granted by means of a subsequent refund so long as refund procedures are applied in a reasonable manner.

The term "beneficial owner" is not defined in the Convention, and is, therefore, defined as under the internal law of the country imposing tax (*i.e.*, the source country). The beneficial owner of the dividend for purposes of Article 10 is the person to which the dividend income is attributable for tax purposes under the laws of the source State. Thus, if a dividend paid by a corporation that is a resident of one of the States (as determined under Article 4 (Residence)) is received by a nominee or agent that is a resident of the other State on behalf of a person that is not a resident of that other State, the dividend is not entitled to the benefits of this Article. However, a dividend received by a nominee on behalf of a resident of that other State would be entitled to benefits. These interpretations are confirmed by paragraph 12 of the Commentary to Article 10 of the OECD Model. See also paragraph 24 of the Commentary to Article 1 of the OECD Model.

Companies holding shares through fiscally transparent entities such as partnerships are considered for purposes of this paragraph to hold their proportionate interest in the shares held by the intermediate entity. As a result, companies holding shares through such entities may be able to claim the benefits of subparagraph (a) under certain circumstances. The lower rate applies when the company's proportionate share of the shares held by the intermediate entity meets the 10 percent threshold. Whether this ownership threshold is satisfied may be difficult to determine and often will require an analysis of the partnership or trust agreement.

The determination of whether the ownership threshold for subparagraph 2(a) is met for purposes of the 5 percent maximum rate of withholding tax is made on the date on which entitlement to the dividend is determined. Thus, in the case of a dividend from a U.S. company, the determination of whether the ownership threshold is met generally would be made on the dividend record date.

Paragraph 3

Paragraph 3 provides exclusive residence-country taxation (*i.e.*, an elimination of withholding tax) with respect to certain dividends distributed by a company that is a resident of one Contracting State to a resident of the other Contracting State. As described further below, this elimination of withholding tax is available with respect to certain inter-company dividends and with respect to tax-exempt pension funds.

Subparagraph (a) of paragraph 3 provides for the elimination of withholding tax on dividends beneficially owned by a company that has owned 80 percent or more of the voting power of the company paying the dividend for the 12-month period ending on the date entitlement to the dividend is determined. The determination of whether the beneficial owner of the dividends owns at least 80 percent of the voting power of the paying company is made by taking into account stock owned both directly and stock owned indirectly through one or more residents of either Contracting State.

6

Eligibility for the elimination of withholding tax provided by subparagraph (a) is subject to additional restrictions based on, but supplementing, the rules of Article 17 (Limitation on Benefits). Accordingly, a company that meets the holding requirements described above will qualify for the benefits of paragraph 3 only if it also: (1) meets the "publicly traded" test of subparagraph 2(c) of Article 17 (Limitation of Benefits), (2) meets the "ownership base erosion" and "active trade or business" test described in subparagraph 2(e) and subparagraph 4 of Article 17 (Limitation of Benefits), (3) meets the "derivative benefits" test of paragraph 3 of Article 17 (Limitation of Benefits), or (4) is granted the benefits of subparagraph 3(a) of Article 10 by the competent authority of the source State pursuant to paragraph 6 of Article 17 (Limitation on Benefits).

These restrictions are necessary because of the increased pressure on the Limitation on Benefits tests resulting from the fact that the United States has relatively few treaties that provide for such elimination of withholding tax on inter-company dividends. The additional restrictions are intended to prevent companies from re-organizing in order to become eligible for the elimination of withholding tax in circumstances where the Limitation on Benefits provision does not provide sufficient protection against treaty-shopping.

For example, assume that ThirdCo is a company resident in a third country that does not have a tax treaty with the United States providing for the elimination of withholding tax on inter-company dividends. ThirdCo owns directly 100 percent of the issued and outstanding voting stock of USCo, a U.S. company, and of SCo, a Swedish company. SCo is a substantial company that manufactures widgets; USCo distributes those widgets in the United States. If ThirdCo contributes to SCo all the stock of USCo, dividends paid by USCo to SCo would qualify for treaty benefits under the active trade or business test of paragraph 4 of Article 17. However, allowing ThirdCo to qualify for the elimination of withholding tax, which is not available to it under the third state's treaty with the United States (if any), would encourage treaty-shopping.

In order to prevent this type of treaty-shopping, paragraph 3 requires SCo to meet the ownership-base erosion requirements of subparagraph 2(e) of Article 17 in addition to the active trade or business test of paragraph 4 of Article 17. Thus, SCo would not qualify for the exemption from withholding tax unless (i) on at least half the days of the taxable year, at least 50 percent of each class of its shares was owned by persons that are residents of Sweden and eligible for treaty benefits under certain specified tests and (ii) less than 50 percent of SCo's gross income is paid in deductible payments to persons that are not residents of either Contracting State. Because SCo is wholly owned by a third country resident, SCo could not qualify for the elimination of withholding tax on dividends from USCo under the ownership-base erosion test and the active trade or business test. Consequently, SCo would need to qualify under another test or obtain discretionary relief from the competent authority under Article 17(6). For purpose of Article 3(a)(ii), it is not sufficient for a company to qualify for treaty benefits generally under the active trade or business test or the ownership-base erosion test unless it qualifies for treaty benefits under both.

Alternatively, companies that are publicly traded or subsidiaries of publicly-traded companies will generally qualify for the elimination of withholding tax. Thus, a company that is a resident of Sweden and that meets the requirements of Article 17(2)(i) or (ii) will be entitled to the elimination of withholding tax, subject to the 12-month holding period requirement of Article 10(3)(a).

In addition, under Article 10(3)(a)(iii), a company that is a resident of a Contracting State may also qualify for the elimination of withholding tax on dividends if it satisfies the derivative benefits test of paragraph 3 of Article 17. Thus, a Swedish company that owns all of the stock of a U.S. corporation may qualify for the elimination of withholding tax if it is wholly-owned, for example, by a U.K., Dutch, or a Mexican publicly-traded company and the other requirements of the derivative benefits test are met. At this time, ownership by companies that are residents of other European Union, European Economic Area or North American Free Trade Agreement countries or that are resident in Switzerland would not qualify the Swedish company for benefits under this provision, as the United States does not have treaties that eliminate the withholding tax on inter-company dividends with any other of those countries. If the United States were to negotiate such treaties with more of those countries, residents of those countries could then qualify as equivalent beneficiaries for purposes of this provision.

The derivative benefits test may also provide benefits to U.S. companies receiving dividends from Swedish subsidiaries, because of the effect of the Parent-Subsidiary Directive in the European Union. Under that directive, inter-company dividends paid within the European Union are free of withholding tax. Under subparagraph (h) of paragraph 7 of Article 17, that directive will also be taken into account in determining whether the owner of a U.S. company receiving dividends from a Swedish company is an "equivalent beneficiary." Thus, a company that is a resident of a member state of the European Union will, by definition, meet the requirements regarding equivalent benefits with respect to any dividends received by its U.S. subsidiary from a Swedish company. For example, assume USCo is a wholly-owned subsidiary of ICo, an Italian publicly-traded company. USCo owns all of the shares of SCo, a Swedish company. If SCo were to pay dividends directly to ICo, those dividends would be exempt from withholding tax in Sweden by reason of the Parent-Subsidiary Directive, even though the tax treaty between Italy and Sweden otherwise would allow Sweden to impose a withholding tax at the rate of 5 percent. If ICo meets the other conditions of subparagraph 7(g) of Article 17, it will be treated as an equivalent beneficiary by reason of subparagraph 7(h) of that article.

A company also may qualify for the elimination of withholding tax pursuant to Article 10(3)(a)(iii) if it is owned by seven or fewer U.S. or Swedish residents who qualify as an "equivalent beneficiary" and meet the other requirements of the derivative benefits provision. This rule may apply, for example, to certain Swedish corporate joint venture vehicles that are closely-held by a few Swedish resident individuals.

Article 10(3) contains a specific rule of application intended to ensure that certain joint ventures, not just wholly-owned subsidiaries, can qualify for benefits. For example, assume that the United States were to enter into a treaty with Country X, a member of the European Union, that includes a provision identical to Article 10(3). USCo is 100 percent owned by SCo, a Swedish company, which in turn is owned 49 percent by PCo, a Swedish publicly-traded company, and 51 percent by XCo, a publicly-traded company that is resident in Country X. In the absence of a special rule for interpreting the derivative benefits provision, each of the shareholders would be treated as owning only their proportionate share of the shares held by SCo. If that rule were applied in this situation, neither shareholder would be an equivalent beneficiary, because neither would meet the 80 percent ownership test with respect to USCo. However, since both PCo and XCo are residents of countries that have treaties with the United States that provide for elimination of withholding tax on inter-company dividends, it is appropriate to provide benefits to SCo in this case.

Consequently, Article 10(3) provides that, when determining whether a person is an equivalent beneficiary, each of the shareholders is treated as owning shares with the same percentage of voting power as the shares held by SCo for purposes of determining whether it would be entitled to an equivalent rate of withholding tax. This rule is necessary because of the high ownership threshold for qualification for the elimination of withholding tax on inter-company dividends.

If a company does not qualify for the elimination of withholding tax under any of the foregoing objective tests, it may request a determination from the relevant competent authority pursuant to paragraph 6 of Article 17. Benefits will be granted with respect to an item of income if the competent authority of the Contracting State in which the income arises determines that the establishment, acquisition or maintenance of such resident and the conduct of its operations did not have as one of its principal purposes the obtaining of benefits under the Convention.

In making its determination under Article 17(6) with respect to income arising in the United States, the U.S. competent authority will consider the obligations imposed upon Sweden by its membership in the European Union. In particular, the United States will have regard for any legal requirements for the facilitation of the free movement of capital among member states of the European Union. The competent authority will also consider the differing internal tax systems, tax incentive regimes and tax treaty practices of the relevant member states.

For example, in the case above where SCo was denied the zero rate of withholding tax because it was wholly owned by ThirdCo, the competent authority would consider whether ThirdCo was a resident of a member state of the European Union or European Economic Area. If it were, that would be a factor in favor of a determination that SCo is entitled to the benefits of the zero rate of withholding tax on dividends. However, that positive factor could be outweighed by negative factors. One negative factor could be a determination by the U.S. competent authority that ThirdCo benefited from a tax incentive regime that eliminated any domestic taxation. The competent authority would also consider facts that might indicate that ThirdCo acquired SCo not "under ordinary business conditions" but instead to interpose SCo between ThirdCo and USCo, creating a Sweden-U.S. "bridge." These might include the fact that existing U.S. operations were restructured in an attempt to benefit from the elimination of withholding tax on dividends; or the fact that ThirdCo was owned by residents of a country that is not a member state of the European Communities. Finally, another significant negative factor would be if the U.S. competent authority faced difficulties in learning the identity of ThirdCo's owners, such as an uncooperative taxpayer or legal barriers such as "economic espionage" or other limitations on the effective exchange of information in the country of which ThirdCo is a resident.

Subparagraph (b) of paragraph 3 of Article 10 of the Convention provides for exclusive taxation by the Contracting State of residence (*i.e.*, the elimination of source-country withholding tax) for dividends beneficially owned by a pension fund (as defined in paragraph 11 of this Article) provided that such dividends are not derived from the carrying on of a business, directly or indirectly, by the pension fund or through an associated enterprise and such fund does not sell or make a contract to sell the holdings from which such dividend is derived within two months of the date the pension fund acquired the holding.

Paragraph 4

Paragraph 4 provides rules for the treatment of dividends paid by RIC or a REIT that are consistent with U.S. treaty policy.

The first sentence of subparagraph 4(a) provides that dividends paid by a RIC or REIT are not eligible for the 5 percent rate of withholding tax of subparagraph 2(a) or the elimination of source-country withholding tax of subparagraph 3(a).

The second sentence of subparagraph 4(a) provides that the 15 percent maximum rate of withholding tax of subparagraph 2(b) applies to dividends paid by RICs and that the elimination of source-country withholding tax of subparagraph 3(b) applies to dividends paid by RICs and beneficially owned by a pension fund.

The third sentence of subparagraph 4(a) provides that the 15 percent rate of withholding tax also applies to dividends paid by a REIT and that the elimination of source-country withholding tax of subparagraph 3(b) applies to dividends paid by REITs and beneficially owned by a pension fund, provided that one of the three following conditions is met. First, the beneficial owner of the dividend is an individual or a pension fund, in either case holding an interest of not more than 10 percent in the REIT. Second, the dividend is paid with respect to a class of stock that is publicly traded and the beneficial owner of the dividend is a person holding an interest of not more than 5 percent of any class of the REIT's shares. Third, the beneficial owner of the dividend holds an interest in the REIT of not more than 10 percent and the REIT is "diversified." A REIT is diversified if the gross value of no single interest in real property held by the REIT exceeds 10 percent of the gross value of the REIT's total interest in real property.

Foreclosure property is not considered an interest in real property, and a REIT holding a partnership interest is treated as owning its proportionate share of any interest in real property held by the partnership.

The restrictions set out above are intended to prevent the use of these entities to gain inappropriate U.S. tax benefits. For example, a company resident in Sweden that wishes to hold a diversified portfolio of U.S. corporate shares could hold the portfolio directly and would bear a U.S. withholding tax of 15 percent on all of the dividends that it receives. Alternatively, it could hold the same diversified portfolio by purchasing 10 percent or more of the interests in a RIC. If the RIC is a pure conduit, there may be no U.S. tax cost to interposing the RIC in the chain of ownership. Absent the special rule in paragraph 4, such use of the RIC could transform portfolio dividends, taxable in the United States under the Convention at a 15 percent maximum rate of withholding tax, into direct investment dividends taxable at a 5 percent maximum rate of withholding tax or eligible for the elimination of source-country withholding tax.

Similarly, a resident of Sweden directly holding U.S. real property would pay U.S. tax upon the sale of the property either at a 30 percent rate of withholding tax on the gross income or at graduated rates on the net income. As in the preceding example, by placing the real property in a REIT, the investor could, absent a special rule, transform income from the sale of real estate into dividend income from the REIT, taxable at the rates provided in Article 10, significantly reducing the U.S. tax that otherwise would be imposed. Paragraph 4 prevents this result and thereby avoids a disparity between the taxation of direct real estate investments and real estate investments made through REIT conduits. In the cases in which paragraph 4 allows a dividend from a REIT to be eligible for the 15 percent rate of withholding tax, the holding in the REIT is not considered the equivalent of a direct holding in the underlying real property.

Paragraph 5

Paragraph 5 provides a broad and flexible definition of the term "dividends." The definition is intended to cover all arrangements that yield a return on an equity investment in a corporation as determined under the tax law of the state of source, including types of arrangements that might be developed in the future.

The term dividends includes income from shares, or other corporate rights that are not treated as debt under the law of the source State, that participate in the profits of the company. The term also includes income that is subjected to the same tax treatment as income from shares by the law of the State of residence of the dividend paying company. Thus, a constructive dividend that results from a non-arm's length transaction between a corporation and a related party is a dividend under paragraph 5.

In the case of the United States, the term dividends includes amounts treated as a dividend under U.S. law upon the sale or redemption of shares or upon a transfer of shares in a reorganization. See, *e.g.*, Rev. Rul. 92-85, 1992-2 C.B. 69 (sale of foreign subsidiary's stock to U.S. sister company is a deemed dividend to extent of subsidiary's and sister's earnings and profits). Further, a distribution from a U.S. publicly traded limited partnership, which is taxed as a corporation under U.S. law, is a dividend for purposes of Article 10. However, a distribution by a limited liability company is not characterized by the United States as a dividend and, therefore, is not a dividend for purposes of Article 10, provided the limited liability company is not taxable as a corporation under U.S. law.

Finally, a payment denominated as interest that is made by a thinly capitalized corporation may be treated as a dividend to the extent that the debt is recharacterized as equity under the laws of the source State. In the case, of the United States, these rules include section 163(j) of the Code.

The term dividends also includes income from arrangements, including debt obligations, carrying the right to participate in profits. In the case of the United States, this includes contingent interest that is not portfolio interest.

Paragraph 6

Paragraph 6 provides that the general source country limitations under paragraph 2 and 3 on dividends do not apply if the beneficial owner of the dividends is a permanent establishment situated in the source country, or performs in that other State independent personal services from a fixed base situated therein, and the dividends are attributable to such permanent establish or fixed base. In such case, the rules of Article 7 (Business Profits) or Article 14 (Independent Personal Service) shall apply, as the case may be. Accordingly, such dividends will be taxed on a net basis using the rates and rules of taxation generally applicable to residents of the Contracting State in which the permanent establishment or fixed base is located, as modified by the Convention. An example of dividends paid with respect to the business property of a permanent establishment would be dividends derived by a dealer in stock or securities from stock or securities that the dealer held for sale to customers.

Paragraph 7

The right of a Contracting State to tax dividends paid by a company that is a resident of the other Contracting State is restricted by paragraph 7 to cases in which the dividends are paid to a resident of that Contracting State or are attributable to a permanent establishment or fixed base in that Contracting State. Thus, a Contracting State may not impose a "secondary" withholding tax on dividends paid by a nonresident company out of earnings and profits from that Contracting State. In the case of the United States, the secondary withholding tax was eliminated for payments made after December 31, 2004 in the American Jobs Creation Act of 2004.

Paragraph 8

Paragraph 8 provides an exemption from U.S. excise taxes on private foundations in the case of a religious, scientific, literary, educational, or charitable organization which is resident in Sweden, but only if such organization has received substantially all of its support from persons other than citizens or residents of the United States. This provision is designed to ensure that the Nobel Foundation, a Swedish charitable organization, will not be subject to U.S. excise taxes.

Paragraphs 9 and 10

Paragraph 9 permits a Contracting State to impose a branch profits tax on a company resident in the other Contracting State. The tax is in addition to other taxes permitted by the Convention. The term "company" is defined in subparagraph 1(b) of Article 3 (General Definitions).

A Contracting State may impose a branch profits tax on a company if the company has income attributable to a permanent establishment in that Contracting State, derives income from real property in that Contracting State that is taxed on a net basis under Article 6 (Income from Real Property), or realizes gains taxable in that State under paragraph 1 of Article 13 (Gains). In the case of the United States, the imposition of such tax is limited, however, to the portion of the aforementioned items of income that represents the amount of such income that is the "dividend equivalent amount." This is consistent with the relevant rules under the U.S. branch profits tax, and the term dividend equivalent amount is defined under U.S. law. Section 884 defines the dividend equivalent amount as an amount for a particular year that is equivalent to the income described above that is included in the corporation's effectively connected earnings and profits for that year, after payment of the corporate tax under Articles 6 (Income from Real Property), 7 (Business Profits) or 13 (Gains), reduced for any increase in the branch's U.S. net equity during the year or increased for any reduction in its U.S. net equity during the year. U.S. net equity is U.S. assets less U.S. liabilities. See Treas. Reg. section 1.884-1.

Sweden currently does not impose a branch profits tax. If Sweden were to impose such a tax, the base is limited to the portion of the income described in subparagraph 9(a) that is comparable to the amount that would be distributed as a dividend by a locally incorporated subsidiary.

Paragraph 10 limits the rate of the branch profits tax allowed under paragraph 9 to 5 percent. Paragraph 10 also provides that the branch profits tax will not be imposed, however, if certain requirements are met. In general, these requirements provide rules for a branch that parallel the rules for when a dividend paid by a subsidiary will be subject to exclusive residence-country taxation (i.e., the elimination of source-country withholding tax). Accordingly, the branch profits tax may not be imposed in the case of a company that: (1) meets the "publicly traded" test of subparagraph 2(c) of Article 17 (Limitation of Benefits), (2) meets the "ownership base erosion" and "active trade or business" test described subparagraph 2(e) and subparagraph 4 of Article 17, (3) meets the "derivative benefits" test of paragraph 3 of Article 17, or (4) is granted the benefits of subparagraph 3(a) of Article 10 by the competent authority pursuant to paragraph 6 of Article 17.

Thus, for example, if a Swedish company would be subject to the branch profits tax with respect to profits attributable to a U.S. branch and not reinvested in that branch, paragraph 10 may apply to eliminate the branch profits tax if the company either met the "publicly traded" test, met both the "ownership-base erosion" *and* "active trade or business" tests, or the derivative benefits test. If, by contrast, a Swedish company did not meet those tests, then the branch profits tax would apply at a rate of 5 percent, unless the Swedish company is granted benefits with respect to the elimination of the branch profits tax by the competent authority pursuant to paragraph 6 of Article 17.

Paragraph 11

Paragraph 11 defines a pension fund to mean a person (as defined in Article 3 (General Definitions)) that is organized under the laws of a Contracting State who is established and maintained in that State primarily to administer or provide pensions or other similar remuneration, including social security payments, and is exempt from tax in that Contracting State with respect to such activities.

Relation to Other Articles

Notwithstanding the foregoing limitations on source country taxation of dividends, the saving clause of paragraph 4 of Article 1 (Personal Scope) permits the United States to tax dividends received by its residents and citizens as if the Convention had not come into effect.

The benefits of this Article are also subject to the provisions of Article 17 (Limitation on Benefits). Thus, if a resident of Sweden is the beneficial owner of dividends paid by a U.S. company, the shareholder must qualify for treaty benefits under at least one of the tests of Article 17 in order to receive the benefits of this Article.

Paragraph 2 of Article III of the Protocol makes a conforming change to the cross-reference in paragraph 5 of Article 24 (Non-Discrimination) of the Convention.

Article V

Article V of the Protocol replaces Article 17 (Limitation on Benefits) of the Convention.

Structure of the Article

Article 17 follows the form used in other recent U.S. income tax treaties. Paragraph 1 states the general rule that a resident of a Contracting State is entitled to benefits otherwise accorded to residents only to the extent that the resident satisfies the requirements of the Article. Paragraph 2 lists a series of attributes of a resident of a Contracting State, any one of which suffices to make such entitled to all the benefits of the Convention. Paragraph 3 provides a so-called "derivative benefits" test under which certain categories of income may qualify for benefits. Paragraph 4 sets forth the active trade or business test, under which a person not entitled to benefits under paragraph 2 may nonetheless be granted benefits with regard to certain types of income. Paragraph 5 provides special rules for so-called "triangular cases" notwithstanding the other provisions of Article 17. Paragraph 6 provides that benefits may also be granted if the competent authority of the State from which the benefits are claimed determines that it is appropriate to grant benefits in that case. Paragraph 7 defines the terms used specifically in this Article.

Even if a person satisfies the requirements of Article 17, benefits shall be granted only if the resident of a Contracting State satisfies any other specified conditions for claiming benefits. This means, for example, that a publicly-traded company that satisfies the conditions of subparagraph 2(c) will be eligible for the elimination of withholding tax on dividends at source only if it also owns 80 percent or more of the voting power of the paying company and satisfies the 12-month holding period requirement of subparagraph 3(a) of Article 10, and satisfies any other conditions specified in Article 10 or any other articles of the Convention.

Paragraph 1

Paragraph 1 provides that a resident of a Contracting State will be entitled to all the benefits of the Convention otherwise accorded to residents of a Contracting State only to the extent provided in this Article.

The benefits otherwise accorded to residents under the Convention include all limitations on source-based taxation, the treaty-based relief from double taxation, and the protection afforded to residents of a Contracting State under Article 24 (Non-Discrimination). Some provisions do not require that a person be a resident in order to enjoy the benefits of those provisions. Article 25 (Mutual Agreement Procedure) is not limited to residents of the Contracting States, and Article 20 (Government Service) applies to government employees regardless of residence. Article 17 accordingly does not limit the availability of treaty benefits under this provisions.

Article 17 and the anti-abuse provisions of domestic law complement each other, as Article 17 effectively determines whether an entity has a sufficient nexus to a Contracting State to be treated as a resident for treaty purposes, while domestic anti-abuse provisions (*e.g.*, business purpose, substance-over-form, step transaction or conduit principles) determine whether a particular transaction should be recast in accordance with its substance. Thus, internal law principles of the source Contracting State may be applied to identify the beneficial owner of an item of income, and Article 17 then will be applied to the beneficial owner to determine if that person is entitled to the benefits of the Convention with respect to such income.

Paragraph 2

Paragraph 2 has five subparagraphs, each of which describes a category of residents that are entitled to all benefits of the Convention. It is intended that the provisions of paragraph 2 will be self-executing. Claiming benefits under paragraph 2 does not require an advance competent authority ruling or approval. The tax authorities may, of course, on review, determine that the taxpayer has improperly interpreted the paragraph and is not entitled to the benefits claimed.

Individuals -- Subparagraph 2(a)

Subparagraph (a) provides that individual residents of a Contracting State will be entitled to all the benefits of the Convention. If such an individual receives income as a nominee on behalf of a third country resident, benefits may be denied under the applicable articles of the Convention by the requirement that the beneficial owner of the income be a resident of a Contracting State.

Governments -- Subparagraph 2(b)

Subparagraph (b) provides that the Contracting States and any political subdivision or local authority thereof will be entitled to all the benefits of the Convention.

Publicly-Traded Corporations -- Subparagraph 2(c)

Subparagraph (c) applies to two categories of companies: publicly traded companies and subsidiaries of publicly traded companies. A company resident in a Contracting State is entitled to all the benefits of the Convention under clause (i) of subparagraph (c) if the principal class of its shares, and any disproportionate class of shares, is regularly traded on one or more recognized stock exchanges and the company satisfies at least one of the following additional requirements. First, the company's principal class of shares is primarily traded on a recognized stock exchange located in a Contracting State of which the company is a resident; or, in the case of a company resident in Sweden, on a recognized stock exchange located within the European Union, any other European Economic Area country or Switzerland; or, in the case of a company resident in the United States, on a recognized stock exchange located in another state that is a party to the North American Free Trade Agreement. Second, the company's primary place of management and control is in its State of residence.

The term "recognized stock exchange" is defined in subparagraph (d) of paragraph 7. It includes the NASDAQ System and any stock exchange registered with the Securities and Exchange Commission as a national securities exchange for purposes of the Securities Exchange Act of 1934. It also includes the Stockholm Stock Exchange, the Nordic Growth Market, and any other exchange subject to regulation by the Swedish Financial Supervisory Authority. The term also includes the Irish Stock Exchange and the stock exchanges of Amsterdam, Brussels, Copenhagen, Frankfurt, Hamburg, Helsinki, London, Madrid, Milan, Oslo, Paris, Reykjavik, Riga, Tallinn, Toronto, Vienna, Vilnius and Zurich, and any other stock exchange agreed upon by the competent authorities of the Contracting States.

The term "principal class of shares" is defined in subparagraph (a) of paragraph 7 to mean the ordinary or common shares of the company representing the majority of the aggregate voting power and value of the company. If the company does not have a class of ordinary or common shares representing the majority of the aggregate voting power and value of the company, then the "principal class of shares" is that class or any combination of classes of shares that represents, in the aggregate, a majority of the voting power and value of the company. In addition, subparagraph (c) of paragraph 7 defines the term "shares" to include depository receipts for shares.

The term "disproportionate class of shares" is defined in subparagraph (b) of paragraph 7. A company has a disproportionate class of shares if it has outstanding a class of shares which is subject to terms or other arrangements that entitle the holder to a larger portion of the company's income, profit, or gain in the other Contracting State than that to which the holder would be entitled in the absence of such terms or arrangements. Thus, for example, a company resident in Sweden meets the test of subparagraph (b) of paragraph 7 if it has outstanding a class of "tracking stock" that pays dividends based upon a formula that approximates the company's return on its assets employed in the United States.

A company whose principal class of shares is regularly traded on a recognized stock exchange will nevertheless not qualify for benefits under subparagraph (c) of paragraph 2 if it has a disproportionate class of shares that is not regularly traded on a recognized stock exchange. The following example illustrates this result.

Example. SCo is a corporation resident in Sweden. SCo has two classes of shares: Common and Preferred. The Common shares are listed and regularly traded on the Stockholm Stock Exchange. The Preferred shares have no voting rights and are entitled to receive dividends equal in amount to interest payments that SCo receives from unrelated borrowers in the United States. The Preferred shares are owned entirely by a single investor that is a resident of a country with which the United States does not have a tax treaty. The Common shares account for more than 50 percent of the value of SCo and for 100 percent of the voting power. Because the owner of the Preferred shares is entitled to receive payments corresponding to the U.S. source interest income earned by SCo, the Preferred shares are a disproportionate class of shares. Because the Preferred shares are not regularly traded on a recognized stock exchange, SCo will not qualify for benefits under subparagraph (c) of paragraph 2.

A class of shares will be "regularly traded" in a taxable year, under subparagraph (e) of paragraph 7, if the aggregate number of shares of that class traded on one or more recognized exchanges during the twelve months ending on the day before the beginning of that taxable year is at least six percent of the average number of shares outstanding in that class during that twelve-month period. For this purpose, if a class of shares was not listed on a recognized stock exchange during this twelve-month period, the class of shares will be treated as regularly traded only if the class meets the aggregate trading requirements for the taxable period in which the income arises. Trading on one or more recognized stock exchanges may be aggregated for purposes of meeting the "regularly traded" standard of subparagraph (e). For example, a U.S. company could satisfy the definition of "regularly traded" through trading, in whole or in part, on a recognized stock exchange located in Sweden or certain third countries. Authorized but unissued shares are not considered for purposes of subparagraph (e).

A company whose principal class of shares is regularly traded on a recognized exchange but cannot meet the primarily traded test may claim treaty benefits if its primary place of management and control is in its country of residence. This test should be distinguished from the "place of effective management" test which is used in the OECD Model and by many other countries to establish residence. In some cases, the place of effective management test has been interpreted to mean the place where the board of directors meets. By contrast, the primary place of management and control test looks to where day-to-day responsibility for the management of the company (and its subsidiaries) is exercised. The company's primary place of management and control will be located in the State in which the company is a resident only if the executive officers and senior management employees exercise day-to-day responsibility for more of the strategic, financial and operational policy decision making for the company (including direct and indirect subsidiaries) in that State than in the other State or any third state, and the staffs that support the management in making those decisions are also based in that State.

A company resident in a Contracting State is entitled to all the benefits of the Convention under clause (ii) of subparagraph (c) of paragraph 2 if five or fewer publicly traded companies described in clause (i) are the direct or indirect owners of at least 50 percent of the aggregate vote and value of the company's shares (and at least 50 percent of any disproportionate class of shares). If the publicly-traded companies are indirect owners, however, each of the intermediate companies must be a resident of one of the Contracting States. Thus, for example, a Swedish company, all the shares of which are owned by another Swedish company, would qualify for benefits under the Convention if the principal class of shares (and any disproportionate classes of shares) of the Swedish parent company are regularly and primarily traded on the London stock exchange. However, a Swedish subsidiary would not qualify for benefits under clause (ii) if the publicly traded parent company were a resident of Ireland, for example, and not a resident of the United States or Sweden. Furthermore, if a Swedish parent company indirectly owned a Swedish company through a chain of subsidiaries, each such subsidiary in the chain, as an intermediate owner, must be a resident of the United States or Sweden for the Swedish subsidiary to meet the test in clause (ii).

Tax-Exempt Organizations and Pensions -- Subparagraph 2(d)

A tax-exempt organization other than a tax-exempt pension fund is entitled to all the benefits of the Convention, without regard to the residence of its beneficiaries or members. Entities qualifying under this subparagraph are those that generally are exempt from tax in their Contracting State of residence and that are established and maintained exclusively to fulfill religious, charitable, educational, scientific, artistic, cultural, or public purposes.

A tax-exempt pension fund is entitled to all the benefits of the Convention if, as of the close of the end of the prior taxable year, more than 50 percent of the beneficiaries, members or participants of the tax-exempt pension are individuals resident in either Contracting State or if the organization sponsoring the tax-exempt pension is entitled to all the benefits of the Convention under Article 17. For purposes of this provision, the term "beneficiaries" should be understood to refer to the persons receiving benefits from the pension fund.

<u>Ownership/Base Erosion -- Subparagraph 2(e)</u>

Subparagraph 2(e) provides an additional method to qualify for treaty benefits that applies to any form of legal entity that is a resident of a Contracting State. The test provided in subparagraph (e), the so-called ownership and base erosion test, is a two-part test. Both prongs of the test must be satisfied for the resident to be entitled to treaty benefits under subparagraph 2(e).

The ownership prong of the test, under clause (i), requires that 50 percent or more of each class of shares or other beneficial interests in the person is owned, directly or indirectly, on at least half the days of the person's taxable year by persons who are residents of the Contracting State of which that person is a resident and that are themselves entitled to treaty benefits under certain parts of paragraph 2 -- subparagraphs (a), (b), (d), or clause (i) of subparagraph (c).

Trusts may be entitled to benefits under this provision if they are treated as residents under Article 4 (Residence) and they otherwise satisfy the requirements of this subparagraph. For purposes of this subparagraph, the beneficial interests in a trust will be considered to be owned by its beneficiaries in proportion to each beneficiary's actuarial interest in the trust. The interest of a remainder beneficiary will be equal to 100 percent less the aggregate percentages held by income beneficiaries. A beneficiary's interest in a trust will not be considered to be owned by a person entitled to benefits under the other provisions of paragraph 2 if it is not possible to determine the beneficiary's actuarial interest. Consequently, if it is not possible to determine the actuarial interest of the beneficiaries in a trust, the ownership test under clause i) cannot be satisfied, unless all possible beneficiaries are persons entitled to benefits under the other subparagraphs of paragraph 2.

The base erosion prong of clause (ii) of subparagraph (e) is satisfied with respect to a person if less than 50 percent of the person's gross income for the taxable year is paid or accrued to persons who are not residents of either Contracting State, in the form of payments deductible for tax purposes in the payer's State of residence. These amounts do not include arm's-length payments in the ordinary course of business for services or tangible property and payments in respect of financial obligations to a bank that is not related to the payor. To the extent they are deductible from the taxable base, trust distributions are deductible payments. However, depreciation and amortization deductions, which do not represent payments or accruals to other persons, are disregarded for this purpose. In the case of Sweden, such amounts do not include the amount of so-called group contributions, if any, paid to a Swedish resident or permanent establishment. Sweden taxes companies on an entity rather than consolidated group basis and therefore, tax consolidation is not allowed. Qualifying companies may exchange group contributions, which are deductible by the payor and taxable to the payee. Through these contributions, tax consolidation can be effectively achieved.

Paragraph 3

Paragraph 3 sets forth a derivative benefits test that is potentially applicable to all treaty benefits, although the test is applied to individual items of income. In general, a derivative benefits test entitles the resident of a Contracting State to treaty benefits if the owner of the resident would have been entitled to the same benefit had the income in question flowed directly to that owner. To qualify under this paragraph, the company must meet an ownership test and a base erosion test.

Subparagraph (a) sets forth the ownership test. Under this test, seven or fewer equivalent beneficiaries must own shares representing at least 95 percent of the aggregate voting power and value of the company and at least 50 percent of any disproportionate class of shares. Ownership may be direct or indirect. The term "equivalent beneficiary" is defined in subparagraph (g) of paragraph 7. This definition may be met in two alternative ways, the first of which has two requirements.

Under the first alternative, a person may be an equivalent beneficiary because it is entitled to equivalent benefits under a treaty between the country of source and the country in which the person is a resident. This alternative has two requirements.

The first requirement is that the person must be a resident of a member state of the European Union, a European Economic Area state, a party to the North American Free Trade Agreement, or Switzerland (collectively, "qualifying States").

The second requirement of the definition of "equivalent beneficiary" is that the person must be entitled to equivalent benefits under an applicable treaty. To satisfy the second requirement, the person must be entitled to all the benefits of a comprehensive treaty between the Contracting State from which benefits of the Convention are claimed and a qualifying State under provisions that are analogous to the rules in paragraph 2 of this Article regarding individuals, qualified governmental entities, publicly-traded companies or entities, and tax-exempt organizations and pensions. If the treaty in question does not have a comprehensive limitation on benefits article, this requirement only is met if the person would be entitled to treaty benefits under the tests in paragraph 2 of this Article applicable to individuals, qualified governmental entities, publicly-traded companies or entities, and tax-exempt organizations and pensions.

In order to satisfy the second requirement necessary to qualify as an "equivalent beneficiary" under paragraph 7(g)(i)(B) with respect to insurance premiums, dividends, interest, royalties or branch tax, the person must be entitled to a rate of excise, withholding or branch tax that is at least as low as the excise, withholding or branch tax rate that would apply under the Convention to such income. Thus, the rates to be compared are: (1) the rate of tax that the source State would have imposed if a qualified resident of the other Contracting State was the beneficial owner of the income; and (2) the rate of tax that the source State would have imposed if the third State resident received the income directly from the source State. For example, USCo is a wholly owned subsidiary of SCo, a company resident in Sweden. SCo is wholly owned by ICo, a corporation resident in Italy. Assuming SCo satisfies the requirements of paragraph 3 of Article 10 (Dividends), SCo would be eligible for the elimination of dividend withholding tax. The dividend withholding tax rate in the treaty between the United States and Italy is 5 percent. Thus, if ICo received the dividend directly from USCo, ICo would have been subject to a 5 percent rate of withholding tax on the dividend. Because ICo would not be entitled to a rate of withholding tax that is at least as low as the rate that would apply under the Convention to such income (*i.e.*, zero), ICo is not an equivalent beneficiary within the meaning of paragraph 7(g)(i) of Article 17 with respect to the elimination of withholding tax on dividends.

Subparagraph 7(h) provides a special rule to take account of the fact that withholding taxes on many inter-company dividends, interest and royalties are exempt within the European Union by reason of various EU directives, rather than by tax treaty. If a U.S. company receives such payments from a Swedish company, and that U.S. company is owned by a company resident in a member state of the European Union that would have qualified for an exemption from withholding tax if it had received the income directly, the parent company will be treated as an equivalent beneficiary. This rule is necessary because many European Union member countries have not re-negotiated their tax treaties to reflect the rates applicable under the directives.

The requirement that a person be entitled to "all the benefits" of a comprehensive tax treaty eliminates those persons that qualify for benefits with respect to only certain types of income. Accordingly, the fact that a French parent of a Swedish company is engaged in the active conduct of a trade or business in France and therefore would be entitled to the benefits of the U.S.-France treaty if it received dividends directly from a U.S. subsidiary of the Swedish company is not sufficient for purposes of this paragraph. Further, the French company cannot be an equivalent beneficiary if it qualifies for benefits only with respect to certain income as a result of a "derivative benefits" provision in the U.S.-France treaty. However, it would be possible to look through the French company to its parent company to determine whether the parent company is an equivalent beneficiary.

The second alternative for satisfying the "equivalent beneficiary" test is available only to residents of one of the two Contracting States. U.S. or Swedish residents who are eligible for treaty benefits by reason of subparagraphs (a), (b), (c)(i), or (d) of paragraph 2 are equivalent beneficiaries for purposes of the relevant tests in Article 17. Thus, a Swedish individual will be an equivalent beneficiary without regard to whether the individual would have been entitled to receive the same benefits if it received the income directly. A resident of a third country cannot qualify for treaty benefits under these provisions by reason of those paragraphs or any other rule of the treaty, and therefore do not qualify as equivalent beneficiaries under this alternative. Thus, a resident of a third country can be an equivalent beneficiary only if it would have been entitled to equivalent benefits had it received the income directly.

The second alternative was included in order to clarify that ownership by certain residents of a Contracting State would not disqualify a U.S. or Swedish company under this paragraph. Thus, for example, if 90 percent of a Swedish company is owned by five companies that are resident in member states of the European Union who satisfy the requirements of clause (i), and 10 percent of the Swedish company is owned by a U.S. or Swedish individual, then the Swedish company still can satisfy the requirements of subparagraph (a) of paragraph 3.

Subparagraph (b) of paragraph 3 sets forth the base erosion test. A company meets this base erosion test if less than 50 percent of its gross income for the taxable period is paid or accrued, directly or indirectly, to a person or persons who are not equivalent beneficiaries in the form of payments deductible for tax purposes in company's State of residence. These amounts do not include arm's-length payments in the ordinary course of business for services or tangible property and payments in respect of financial obligations to a bank that is not related to the payor. This test is the same as the base erosion test in clause (ii) of subparagraph (e) of paragraph 2, except that deductible payments made to equivalent beneficiaries, rather than amounts paid to residents of a Contracting State, are not counted against a company for purposes of determining whether the company exceeded the 50 percent limit.

As in the case of base erosion test in subparagraph (e) of paragraph 2, deductible payments in subparagraph (b) of paragraph 3 also do not include arm's length payments in the ordinary course of business for services or tangible property or with respect to financial obligations to banks that are residents of either Contracting State.

Paragraph 4

Paragraph 4 sets forth a test under which a resident of a Contracting State that does not qualify for treaty benefits under paragraph 2 may receive treaty benefits with respect to certain items of income that are connected to an active trade or business conducted in its State of residence.

Subparagraph (a) sets forth the general rule that a resident of a Contracting State engaged in the active conduct of a trade or business in that State may obtain the benefits of the Convention with respect to an item of income, profit, or gain derived in the other Contracting State. The item of income, profit, or gain, however, must be derived in connection with or incidental to that trade or business.

The term "trade or business" is not defined in the Convention. Pursuant to paragraph 2 of Article 3 (General Definitions), when determining whether a resident of Sweden is entitled to the benefits of the Convention under paragraph 4 of this Article with respect to an item of income derived from sources within the United States, the United States will ascribe to this term the meaning that it has under the law of the United States. Accordingly, the U.S. competent authority will refer to the regulations issued under section 367(a) for the definition of the term "trade or business." In general, therefore, a trade or business will be considered to be a specific unified group of activities that constitute or could constitute an independent economic enterprise carried on for profit. Furthermore, a corporation generally will be considered to carry on a trade or business only if the officers and employees of the corporation conduct substantial managerial and operational activities.

The business of making or managing investments for the resident's own account will be considered to be a trade or business only when part of banking, insurance or securities activities conducted by a bank, an insurance company, or a registered securities dealer. Such activities conducted by a person other than a bank, insurance company or registered securities dealer will not be considered to be the conduct of an active trade or business, nor would they be considered to be the conduct of an active trade or business if conducted by a bank, insurance company or registered securities dealer but not as part of the company's banking, insurance or dealer business.

An item of income is derived in connection with a trade or business if the income-producing activity in the State of source is a line of business that "forms a part of" or is "complementary" to the trade or business conducted in the State of residence by the income recipient.

A business activity generally will be considered to form part of a business activity conducted in the State of source if the two activities involve the design, manufacture or sale of the same products or type of products, or the provision of similar services. The line of business in the State of residence may be upstream, downstream, or parallel to the activity conducted in the State of source. Thus, the line of business may provide inputs for a manufacturing process that occurs in the State of source, may sell the output of that manufacturing process, or simply may sell the same sorts of products that are being sold by the trade or business carried on in the State of source.

Example 1. USCo is a corporation resident in the United States. USCo is engaged in an active manufacturing business in the United States. USCo owns 100 percent of the shares of SCo, a company resident in Sweden. SCo distributes USCo products in Sweden. Because the business activities conducted by the two corporations involve the same products, SCo's distribution business is considered to form a part of USCo's manufacturing business.

Example 2. The facts are the same as in Example 1, except that USCo does not manufacture. Rather, USCo operates a large research and development facility in the United States that licenses intellectual property to affiliates worldwide, including SCo. SCo and other USCo affiliates then manufacture and market the USCo-designed products in their respective markets. Because the activities conducted by SCo and USCo involve the same product lines, these activities are considered to form a part of the same trade or business.

For two activities to be considered to be "complementary," the activities need not relate to the same types of products or services, but they should be part of the same overall industry and be related in the sense that the success or failure of one activity will tend to result in success or failure for the other. Where more than one trade or business is conducted in the State of source and only one of the trades or businesses forms a part of or is complementary to a trade or business conducted in the State of residence, it is necessary to identify the trade or business to which an item of income is attributable. Royalties generally will be considered to be derived in connection with the trade or business to which the underlying intangible property is attributable. Dividends will be deemed to be derived first out of earnings and profits of the treaty-benefited trade or business, and then out of other earnings and profits. Interest income may be allocated under any reasonable method consistently applied. A method that conforms to U.S. principles for expense allocation will be considered a reasonable method.

Example 3. Americair is a corporation resident in the United States that operates an international airline. SSub is a wholly-owned subsidiary of Americair resident in Sweden. SSub operates a chain of hotels in Sweden that are located near airports served by Americair flights. Americair frequently sells tour packages that include air travel to Sweden and lodging at SSub hotels. Although both companies are engaged in the active conduct of a trade or business, the businesses of operating a chain of hotels and operating an airline are distinct trades or businesses. Therefore SSub's business does not form a part of Americair's business. However, SSub's business is considered to be complementary to Americair's business because they are part of the same overall industry (travel), and the links between their operations tend to make them interdependent.

Example 4. The facts are the same as in Example 3, except that SSub owns an office building in Sweden instead of a hotel chain. No part of Americair's business is conducted through the office building. SSub's business is not considered to form a part of or to be complementary to Americair's business. They are engaged in distinct trades or businesses in separate industries, and there is no economic dependence between the two operations.

Example 5. USFlower is a company resident in the United States. USFlower produces and sells flowers in the United States and other countries. USFlower owns all the shares of SHolding, a corporation resident in Sweden. SHolding is a holding company that is not engaged in a trade or business. SHolding owns all the shares of three corporations that are resident in Sweden: SFlower, SLawn, and SFish. SFlower distributes USFlower flowers under the USFlower trademark in Sweden. SLawn markets a line of lawn care products in Sweden under the USFlower trademark. In addition to being sold under the same trademark, SLawn and SFlower products are sold in the same stores and sales of each company's products tend to generate increased sales of the other's products. SFish imports fish from the United States and distributes it to fish wholesalers in Sweden. For purposes of paragraph 4, the business of SFlower forms a part of the business of USFlower, the business of SLawn is complementary to the business of USFlower, and the business of SFish is neither part of nor complementary to that of USFlower.

An item of income derived from the State of source is "incidental to" the trade or business carried on in the State of residence if production of the item facilitates the conduct of the trade or business in the State of residence. An example of incidental income is the temporary investment of working capital of a person in the State of residence in securities issued by persons in the State of source.

Subparagraph (b) of paragraph 4 states a further condition to the general rule in subparagraph (a) in cases where the trade or business generating the item of income in question is carried on either by the person deriving the income or by any associated enterprises. Subparagraph (b) states that the trade or business carried on in the State of residence, under these circumstances, must be substantial in relation to the activity in the State of source. The substantiality requirement is intended to prevent a narrow case of treaty-shopping abuses in which a company attempts to qualify for benefits by engaging in de minimis connected business activities in the treaty country in which it is resident (*i.e.*, activities that have little economic cost or effect with respect to the company business as a whole).

The determination of substantiality is made based upon all the facts and circumstances and takes into account the comparative sizes of the trades or businesses in each Contracting State (measured by reference to asset values, income and payroll expenses), the nature of the activities performed in each Contracting State, and the relative contributions made to that trade or business in each Contracting State. In any case, in making each determination or comparison, due regard will be given to the relative sizes of the U.S. and Swedish economies.

The determination in subparagraph (b) also is made separately for each item of income derived from the State of source. It therefore is possible that a person would be entitled to the benefits of the Convention with respect to one item of income but not with respect to another. If a resident of a Contracting State is entitled to treaty benefits with respect to a particular item of income under paragraph 4, the resident is entitled to all benefits of the Convention insofar as they affect the taxation of that item of income in the State of source.

The application of the substantiality requirement only to income from related parties focuses only on potential abuse cases, and does not hamper certain other kinds of non-abusive activities, even though the income recipient resident in a Contracting State may be very small in relation to the entity generating income in the other Contracting State. For example, if a small U.S. research firm develops a process that it license to a very large, unrelated, Swedish pharmaceutical manufacturer, the size of the U.S. research firm would not have to be tested against the size of the Swedish manufacturer. Similarly, a small U.S. bank that makes a loan to a very large unrelated Swedish business would not have to pass a substantiality test to receive treaty benefits under Paragraph 4.

Subparagraph (c) of paragraph 4 provides special rules for determining whether a resident of a Contracting State is engaged in the active conduct of a trade or business within the meaning of subparagraph (a). Subparagraph (c) attributes the activities of a partnership to each of its partners. Subparagraph (c) also attributes to a person activities conducted by persons "connected" to such person. A person ("X") is connected to another person ("Y") if X possesses 50 percent or more of the beneficial interest in Y (or if Y possesses 50 percent or more of the beneficial interest in X). For this purpose, X is connected to a company if X owns shares representing fifty percent or more of the aggregate voting power and value of the company or fifty percent or more of the beneficial equity interest in the company. X also is connected to Y if a third person possesses fifty percent or more of the beneficial interest in both X and Y. For this purpose, if X or Y is a company, the threshold relationship with respect to such company or companies is fifty percent or more of the aggregate voting power and value or fifty percent or more of the beneficial equity interest. Finally, X is connected to Y if, based upon all the facts and circumstances, X controls Y, Y controls X, or X and Y are controlled by the same person or persons.

Paragraph 5

Paragraph 5 deals with the treatment of insurance premiums, royalties and interest in the context of a so-called "triangular case."

The term "triangular case" refers to the use of the following structure by a resident of Sweden to earn, in this case, interest income from the United States. The resident of Sweden, who is assumed to qualify for benefits under one or more of the provisions of Article 17 (Limitation on Benefits), sets up a permanent establishment in a third jurisdiction that imposes only a low rate of tax on the income of the permanent establishment. The Swedish resident lends funds into the United States through the permanent establishment. The permanent establishment, despite its third-jurisdiction location, is an integral part of a Swedish resident. Therefore the income that it earns on those loans, absent the provisions of paragraph 5, is entitled to exemption from U.S. withholding tax under the Convention. Under a current Swedish income tax treaty with the host jurisdiction of the permanent establishment, the income of the permanent establishment is exempt from Swedish tax. Thus, the interest income is exempt from U.S. tax, is subject to little tax in the host jurisdiction of the permanent establishment, and is exempt from Swedish tax.

Because the United States does not exempt the profits of a third-jurisdiction permanent establishment of a U.S. resident from U.S. tax, either by statute or by treaty, the paragraph only applies with respect to U.S. source insurance premiums, interest, or royalties that are attributable to a third-jurisdiction permanent establishment of a Swedish resident.

Paragraph 5 replaces the otherwise applicable rules in the Convention for insurance premiums, interest and royalties with a 15 percent U.S. withholding tax for interest and royalties and the rules of U.S. domestic law for insurance premiums under the following circumstances. First, the actual tax paid on the U.S. source premiums, interest or royalties in the third state is subject is less than 60 percent of the tax that would have been payable in Sweden if the income were earned in Sweden by the enterprise and were not attributable to the permanent establishment in the third state.

In general, the principles employed under Code section 954(b)(4) will be employed to determine whether the profits are subject to an effective rate of taxation that is above the specified threshold.

Notwithstanding the level of tax on interest and royalty income of the permanent establishment, paragraph 5 will not apply under certain circumstances. In the case of interest (as defined in Article 11(Interest)), paragraph 5 will not apply if the interest is derived in connection with, or is incidental to, the active conduct of a trade or business carried on by the permanent establishment in the third state. The business of making, managing or simply holding investments is not considered to be an active trade or business, unless these are banking or securities activities carried on by a bank or registered securities dealer. In the case of royalties, paragraph 5 will not apply if the royalties are received as compensation for the use of, or the right to use, intangible property produced or developed by a permanent establishment itself.

Paragraph 6

Paragraph 6 provides that a resident of one of the States that is not entitled to the benefits of the Convention as a result of paragraphs 1 through 5 still may be granted benefits under the Convention at the discretion of the competent authority of the State from which benefits are claimed. In making determinations under paragraph 6, that competent authority will take into account as its guideline whether the establishment, acquisition, or maintenance of the person seeking benefits under the Convention, or the conduct of such person's operations, has or had as one of its principal purposes the obtaining of benefits under the Convention. Thus, persons that establish operations in one of the States with a principal purpose of obtaining the benefits of the Convention ordinarily will not be granted relief under paragraph 6.

The competent authority may determine to grant all benefits of the Convention, or it may determine to grant only certain benefits. For instance, it may determine to grant benefits only with respect to a particular item of income in a manner similar to paragraph 4. Further, the competent authority may set time limits on the duration of any relief granted.

For purposes of implementing paragraph 6, a taxpayer will be permitted to present his case to the relevant competent authority for an advance determination based on the facts. In these circumstances, it is also expected that if the competent authority determines that benefits are to be allowed, they will be allowed retroactively to the time of entry into force of the relevant treaty provision or the establishment of the structure in question, whichever is later.

A competent authority is required by paragraph 6 to consult the other competent authority before denying benefits under this paragraph. According to the notes, the competent authority will consider the obligations of Sweden by virtue of its membership in the European Union in making a determination under paragraph 6. In particular, the competent authority will consider any legal requirements for the facilitation of the free movement of capital and persons, together with the differing internal tax systems, tax incentive regimes and existing tax treaty policies among member states of the European Union. As a result, where certain changes in circumstances otherwise might cause a person to cease to be a eligible for treaty benefits under paragraphs 2 of Article 17, for example, such changes need not result in the denial of benefits.

The changes in circumstances contemplated include, all under ordinary business conditions, a change in the State of residence of a major shareholder of a company; the sale of part of the stock of a Swedish company to a resident in another member state of the European Union; or an expansion of a company's activities in other member states of the European Union. So long as the relevant competent authority is satisfied that those changed circumstances are not attributable to tax avoidance motives, they will count as a factor favoring the granting of benefits under paragraph 6, if consistent with existing treaty policies, such as the need for effective exchange of information.

Paragraph 7

Paragraph 7 defines several key terms for purposes of Article 17. Each of the defined terms is discussed in the context in which it is used.

Article VI

The Protocol adds an additional paragraph to Article 20 (Government Services) of the Convention. This paragraph provides a grandfather rule to eliminate the unintended consequences resulting from the 1994 U.S.-Sweden income tax treaty regarding the taxation of local employees (or former employees) of the Embassy in Stockholm and consulate in Gothenburg.

The 1939 U.S.-Sweden income tax treaty generally provided that wages, salaries and similar compensation and pensions paid by one Contracting State to individuals in another Contracting State were exempt from tax in the latter State. The U.S. government reduced the salaries paid to Swedish residents and citizens working at the U.S. Embassy in Stockholm or consulate in Gothenburg to take account of the fact that they were exempt from Swedish income tax. Accordingly, their pensions, which were based on "high-three," were also reduced.

The 1994 U.S.-Sweden income tax treaty generally provides that remuneration (other than a pension) paid by a Contracting State to an individual in respect of services rendered to that State is taxable only that State unless the person was already a resident of the other State before he began working for the first-mentioned State. The 1994 treaty also generally provides that a pension paid by a Contracting State to an individual in respect of services to that State are taxable only in the other Contracting State if the individual is a resident and citizen of that State.

Under the 1994 U.S.-Sweden tax treaty, Sweden does tax the pensions of Swedish residents or citizens who worked in the U.S. Embassy in Stockholm and consulate in Gothenburg. The 1994 U.S.-Sweden tax treaty failed to provide a grandfather for former employees whose pension benefits are based on a "high three" that took into account the exemption from Swedish income tax provided for in the 1939 U.S.-Sweden tax, thereby significantly reducing the expected benefits to these former employees.

To rectify this problem, the Protocol adds an additional paragraph to Article 20 (Government Service) of the Convention to provide that Sweden may not tax a pension under the U.S. Civil Service Retirement Pension Plan paid by the United States to employees of the U.S. embassy in Stockholm or the U.S. consulate general in Gothenburg if the individual was hired prior to 1978.

Article VII

The Protocol makes conforming changes to Article 23 (Relief from Double Taxation) to reflect the amendments made to the saving clause of paragraph 4 Article 1 (Personal Scope) and to reflect amendments to section 877 of the Code in 1996.

Article VIII

Article VIII of the Protocol contains the rules for bringing the Protocol into force and giving effect to its provisions.

Paragraph 1 provides for the ratification of the Convention by both Contracting States according to their applicable procedures. Each State must notify the other as soon as its requirements for ratification have been complied with. The Convention will enter into force on the thirtieth day after the later of such notifications accompanied by an instrument of ratification.

In the United States, the process leading to ratification and entry into force is as follows: Once a protocol or treaty has been signed by authorized representatives of the two Contracting States, the Department of State sends the protocol or treaty to the President who formally transmits it to the Senate for its advice and consent to ratification, which requires approval by two-thirds of the Senators present and voting. Prior to this vote, however, it generally has been the practice of the Senate Committee on Foreign Relations to hold hearings on the protocol or treaty and make a recommendation regarding its approval to the full Senate. Both Government and private sector witnesses may testify at these hearings. After receiving the Senate's advice and consent to ratification, the protocol or treaty is returned to the President for his signature on the ratification document. The President's signature on the document completes the process in the United States.

The date on which a treaty enters into force is not necessarily the date on which its provisions take effect. Paragraph 2 contains rules that determine when the provisions of the treaty will have effect.

Under subparagraphs (a)(i) and (b)(ii), the provisions of the Protocol relating to taxes withheld at source will have effect with respect to amounts paid or credited on or after the first day of the second month next following the date on which the Protocol enters into force. For example, if instruments of ratification are exchanged on April 25 of a given year, the withholding rates specified in paragraphs 2 and 3 of Article 10 (Dividends) would be applicable to any dividends paid or credited on or after June 1 of that year. Similarly, the revised Limitation on Benefits provisions of Article 5 of the Protocol would apply with respect to any payments of interest, royalties or other amounts on which withholding would apply under the Code if those amounts are paid or credited on or after June 1.

This rule allows the benefits of the withholding reductions to be put into effect as soon as possible, without waiting until the following year. The delay of one to two months is required to allow sufficient time for withholding agents to be informed about the change in withholding rates. If for some reason a withholding agent withholds at a higher rate than that provided by the Convention (perhaps because it was not able to re-program its computers before the payment is made), a beneficial owner of the income that is a resident of Sweden may make a claim for refund pursuant to section 1464 of the Code.

Under subparagraph (b)(i) the provision of Article VI of the Protocol relating to the taxation of pensions of certain employees of the U.S. embassy in Stockholm or the U.S. consulate general in Gothenburg by Sweden is effective for income derived on or after January 1, 1996.

For all other taxes, subparagraphs (a)(ii) and (b)(iii) specify that the Protocol will have effect for any taxable period beginning on or after January 1 of the year next following entry into force.